About the Author

Beverly was born in England. After working as a youth leader she married and in 1981 moved to Tel Aviv. There she has been involved in the family print business as production manager since its establishment in 1984. Beverly has always enjoyed writing and has written poetry for many years. Her other interests include cooking and travelling.

Dedicated to Barry with love

Beverly Green

CAUGHT IN THE LIGHT

AUSTIN MACAULEY
PUBLISHERS LTD.

ISBN 9781785543166 (paperback)
ISBN 9781785543173 (eBook)

www.austinmacauley.com

First Published (2016)
Austin Macauley Publishers Ltd.
25 Canada Square
Canary Wharf
London
E14 5LQ

Acknowledgments

If you've chosen this over another book

If you've troubled to stop and take a look

If you've paid good money to take me home

Consider this an acknowledgment to you alone

Contents

Chapter One – Dark

Caught in the Light	14
The Field	15
You're Already There	16
Time	17
On Innocence	18
My Conscience	19
A Fond Farewell	20
Battle Ground	21
Accidents	22
Burning Bridges	23
Coma	24
Fireflies	25
Ethereal Heights	26
Flight	27
Friendship	28
Icarus	29
Loss	30
Misunderstood	31
Safe Harbour	32
See of Mist	33
Alzheimer's	34
The Book	35
Moonbeams	36
The Means to an End	37
Palette	38
Peace	39
Nothing Left	40
Shared Senses	41
The Four Winds	42
Desertion	43
Ride of My Life	44
You're My Bookend Lover	45
SOS	46
To and Fro	47
Brimming	48
Fountain	49
Super Dad	50
Freedom	51
Hollywood Heroes Die	52
The Comforter	53
Wise Words	54
Chocolate Box	55

Re-Gifting   56
Stand Up and be Counted   57
Gravestone   58
Muddy Waters   59
On Weakness   60
Grind   61
The Tramp   62
Happiness at Home   63
Under Pressure   64

Chapter Two - Light

The Boss   66
My Ex   67
Sun Down / Sun Up   68
A Tired Man's Woes   69
Order   70
Someone Out There   71
Who is She?   72
Truth   73
The Hunter   74
Sweet Old Lady   75
Spot   77
Liar!   78
On Tears   79
Wishing Well   80
The Fortune Teller   81
Professionalism   82
1960s   83
The Psychiatrist's Misery   84
Constructive Criticism   85
Boredom   86
Burn Baby Burn   87
The Secret's Out!   88
Health Food?   89
Future   90
The King's Game   91
Doctor's Advice   92
Gossip   93
Lovers' Games   94
Left or Right   95
It's Hell in Heaven   96
The Debutante Dress   97
Do as You're Told   98
Heavenly   99
Blind as a Bat   100
Silent Movies   101
Teamwork   102
Scotch for the Scotsman   103

Who Needs Them?   104
Beautiful Creature   105
Internet Advice   106
Man of my Dreams   107
The Fisherman   108
Pot of Gold   109

CHAPTER ONE

DARK

Caught in the Light

A creamy marble in the inky black sky
Stares down at me, an unblinking eye,
I'm scared that night has come too soon
The sun sold my secret to the moon.

Dispensing cold judgment over my day
Hungry for the debt I'll be made to pay,
There's no sanctuary from a waxing beam
Caught in the snare of its milky stream.

Crystal tears streak down my pale cheek,
Suffocated with fear it's hard to speak,
I face the accuser, to plead my case
So maybe tomorrow I'll be shown some grace.

A judgmental moon has now left the sky,
The traitorous usurper having risen high
Baring down on me with its scalding heat,
Keen to lay punishment at my feet...

Confiding in the sun that I'd once strayed,
It promised to always leave me some shade.
So remember! Be cautious in whom you confide,
One day they may go over to the other side.

The Field

A threatening sky pasted with black choking clouds
Brings a menacing evil that crawls in overhead,
We are helpless now, shrouded in its ominous cloak.
Creeping across the landscape the predator takes hold
Swallowing the ground, devouring all on its charted course
The rumbling fearless giant commands and nature obeys.
A scarecrow's torn hat shoots across the desolate land
His face expressionless, a stiff body pummelled by the wind.
No crows to scare from the fields, no sparrows to pick his brain.
He waits patiently for the devilish darkness to pass overhead
Knowing the climax of the oncoming storm is about to explode.
Clouds violently erupt, empting their swollen bellies,
Wet spears stab at the hard cracked ground,
Deflected, returning again, eagerly drunk by a parched soil.
The thirsting drought stricken earth now soothed and healed
Light returns, the cycle of life continues on its journey.

You're Already There

A log cabin, a grassy slope, a stream, this is my haven,
Swathed in calmness I become absorbed by a stunning peace.
It is a peace that erases the turmoil of a harsh world beyond.
Fragrance from wild flowers waft through the heady spring air,
Masking choking fumes of the frenetic urban day that is my life.
As I become refreshed, intoxicated by pure cool water,
The city stench of alcoholic blindness dissipates before me.
Shunning the escalating violence, a force of nature takes its place,
The desperate need for wealth vigorously evicted; an unwanted tenant.
Too soon the serenity of this treasured moment evaporates.
Helplessly I watch the vision dissolve before my weary eyes
The cabin's logs unravel as a snagged thread from a sweater.
Tumbling down the hill they crash into water,
The deep emerald carpet crushed by their pounding weight.
Clear waters muddy, the current accelerates, the stench returns,
Swiftly I'm carried back into the stream of mechanization…
Smoothing a hand gently across the surface of my wooden desk
I conjure up the echoes of a parallel paradise, just beyond my grasp.

Time

Time has cast its heavy shadow, the light is fading
Seconds, minutes and hours, lost moments.
A veracious companion, nourished by our lives
An enemy that holds our youthful dreams in check.
But then we are freed!
Misled into believing we are masters of our fate
The eternal partner beguiles us with distractions
Seconds are lost, and the hours close in.
Days dissolve, each one rolling away,
Pearls from the thread of a breaking necklace
Racing across the floor, impossible to hold.
For a fleeting moment we have the upper hand
Passing across into the white light of eternity
At last, rid of that damning ticking clock...
Still in our absence there is no escape,
Forever branded by the time since our passing.

On Innocence

A golden treasure, anchored in the pool of life
Shimmering beneath the surface beckons.
Many pass by with outstretched hands,
They scheme; plotting how to capture the glittering prize?
A child with pure heart, undaunted,
Plunges in a spontaneous dive to pursue the dream.
Reaching out, he clutches the treasure close to his heart,
Emerging from the pool, glowing with breathless wonder.
Gazing down on the wooden block he is filled with naïve hope.
The passers by now deny it was ever their desire
But a child with a pure heart and imagination
Adds it to the fire of life and is warmed by its flames.

My Conscience

I watch you expectantly from a distance,
Hovering in the shadows…
My personal observation
A meditation of deep absorption.
I breathe in the air where you have just passed and sigh.
Oblivious of my existence, I hold your pace, trace your steps.
So many times I have cried out, but you are deaf to my voice.
Stop for a while so we may become companions
I know you so well; the time has come for you to know me.

A Fond Farewell

A church full of people,
Gathered to say goodbye
Each dressed in black,
Solemn and reflective.

One by one their echoing
Footsteps approach,
All with a desperate need
To say an intimate farewell.

Beneath her veil a tearful wife,
Sighing with relief, no more lies
By her side a child inwardly smiling,
No more senseless beatings.

A dutiful brother head hung in prayer,
Praying for inheritance.
Across the aisle a stoic business partner,
Coldly calculating the benefits.

The disassociated vicar stands silent,
Bored beyond even his belief!
But there was one who loved him
One who stayed away.

Battle Ground

This is my war, this is my fight!
Lines drawn in the sand.
I fed you with comfort, dressed you in pleasure,
Led you along the path of happiness,
There you coldly turned away
Not once glancing back, casting me aside,
A searing hot coal.
We stand now on opposing sides;
You have cast the first blow.
Now my turn has come
I will be unforgiving,
With my strategy carved out,
Poised to wear you down.
Unaware of when I'll strike,
Or what revenge has been set in motion.
The scales of love and hate
Are weighted against you.
This is my war, this is my fight!
Lines drawn in the sand.

Accidents

Accidents will happen; they happen all the time
Eve really should have understood, the apple was a sign
Didn't she know better, than to listen to the snake?
An innocent in The Garden? A critical mistake!
What was so enticing about the fruit of the forbidden tree?
Wanting to impress him she assumed no one could see...
But after tasting the sweetness, bitterness soon seeped in
Now aware there was a cost, and a penalty for her sin.
So if you're guilty of deceiving, having given another your word
Think how to hide evidence so it will never be seen or heard!

Burning Bridges

Standing across the deep river watching,
A burning wooden bridge dissolves into ash.
Scorching flames stinging from across the water,
Fiery hands with biting fingers reach out to me.
Thick black smoke darkens the clear blue sky above,
Too late to mend, too early to seek another crossing,
There is no way back for me, none forward for you.
The charred match you are clutching has soiled your hand.
Maybe before today I would have swum back to you,
Perhaps built another bridge, more resilient to fire,
But there are no more trees in our forest left to fell,
And I no longer have strength to repair your damage.

Coma

Don't leave!
I'm just pretending to be asleep
My eyes shut tight, breathing deep
I can hear the muffled voices speak
How I've been laying here for a week

Debating the strength of medication
To sink me into deeper sedation!
Questioning as to the dose of the drip
And off into oblivion let me slip.

I don't remember that much at all
Of how and when I had my fall
Plummeting like a timbering tree
Crashing to earth so helplessly.

They're muttering more about my head
And how I must be almost dead
I try to tell them I'll wake up soon
But they've dimmed the lights and left the room.

Fireflies

Fireflies illuminate my mind
Ideas that hover, settle, move on
Imagination sparked, ideas that shine
Fireflies illuminate my mind

Rainbows paint my imagination
Tints mingle and colour my dreams
A backdrop of spangled light
Rainbows paint my imagination

But shadows creep into my thoughts
Veiled darkness shrouds my vision
Moving silently through my world
Shadows creep into my thoughts

Fireflies disappear as the day begins
Rainbows slowly melt away
Shadows are extinguished by the night
But I still sense them all.

Ethereal Heights

Looking down from ethereal heights on shards of the day,
Everything distorted, tainted and out of focus.
All semblance of order has become dispersed
What happened to your life that dripped with optimism?
Too much time wasted, too much time passed.
My words tumble into the void.
Opiates have dulled the sharp corners of your mind,
The warning flares shot high into a sky of possibilities
Dissolve unheeded, you are disinterested.
Your chosen path has led you into chaos
But I will not let go and you must not give in.

Flight

Gazing out of the small window
I imagine myself waltzing across the clouds
Gliding from one white puff to another,
Floating back and forth in easy motion.
Glancing across the aisle, a fellow traveller,
A dozing, unsupported head snaps up.
Dribble down his jaw, a floppy head drops again,
His shirt, a stained mixture of sweat and in-flight food.
Quickly! Go back outside!
Out there on my own, a journey of freedom
Increasing my speed I move across the sky
Complete and perfect silence.
"This is the captain speaking" brings me back
I don't care about details of the flight path!
I don't care what the local time is at my destination!
Wheels down, brakes on, arrival hall.
Gazing through another window I peer out of the taxi
Quickly! Go back outside!
For a fleeting moment up in the clouds
I catch a glimpse of a carefree spirit never going home.

Friendship

In a forest of confusing thoughts looking for the light
The darkness overwhelming, you lost the strength to fight.
In the muddy depths of fear you grasped at a damaged tree,
It soon became an anchor, your rock in a raging sea.
The trunk was old and weary with roots in some decay,
But this worn friend supported you and helped to guide the way.
Then by your feet you noticed, growing on unsure ground
A small green shoot of hope appeared, safe haven had been found
Among the chaos of your mind your thoughts began to clear
You surely would soon see again and lose that senseless fear
So now when there's darkness, and everything seems insane
I am your constant companion; you'll never be alone again.

Icarus

We are all Icarus, our laboured flights on weighted wings,
Powerful energies pulling us up towards our own magnetic suns.
Youthfulness counterbalancing burdens strapped to our backs
Ideas, hopes and desires melded as one commanding force.
Beware! Hastily constructed arcs ensure a swift demise,
Scale back your vain attempt at a meteoric rise above others
Watch for the dripping wax and the feathers that stray, heed their sign.

Loss

The sun stopped shining yesterday, the atmosphere held no air
The heavy weight of anxiety, filled me with despair
Empty rain clouds passing through the darkness of the sky
The taste for life now drained from me, leaving my days dry
So much love and passion that moved us every day
We didn't notice in our rush that time had slipped away.
Who'd have thought it would come to this, such a painful end
Fate was cruel and unforgiving as it robbed me of my friend.
The world turned dark as you travelled off, into the unknown
My banshee cries ricochet around our empty home.
They say that as the time goes by, the wound will slowly heal
Platitudes and a few kind words now make my life surreal.
Maybe again there'll be happiness sometime along the way
But as for now my heavy heart cannot see that day.

Misunderstood

First a loud scream, then a blood curdling yell
Some poor creature was tormented in hell
Nobody came to help the poor child
Their torturous screaming frantic and wild
A menacing darkness shrouded her bed
As if demons and dragons fought in her head
Suffocated with panic and drenched in tears
She flayed like a madman struggling with fears
The light snapped on so she hid her face
The way she'd behaved had been a disgrace
Her best friend, confiscated by her mother
To teach her to share the doll with her brother
She had thought it was strange for such a toy
To be shared with him as he was a boy
She couldn't perceive still hidden away
Her baby brother had been born gay
In years to come during the dark of night
With his own demons he'd have to fight
His sister now understood the torture was his
Not a concept she'd grasped when they were kids.

Safe Harbour

The wind has lifted my sails again, spiriting me along
I thought this would never happen, once that you had gone.
The dark green ocean with its swell, pushing me on my way
Will not let me float in depression, for yet another day.
You never boarded the ship again, when I had to leave the port
Having waited long weeks for you, thirsting for your support.
At the time it seemed to be, the only choice to make
Traveling off on my own, leaving you in my wake
For what seemed an eternity I drifted with no course
Avoided all familiar ports, like a repelling, magnetic force
There were a few that sailed close by, trying to come aboard
But I fired out warning shots that could not be ignored.
Still, how much time can a person bear, to float alone at sea?
At some time we all need safe harbour, where ever that may be.
White seagulls hover up above, announcing I've returned
A crying fanfare, sounding out, the lesson that I'd learned.

See of Mist

There is a fine wet mist suspended in the air
The translucent curtain hangs motionless.
My spatial perception now faltering leaves me,
Opaque and suffocating it has become a heavy fog.
The spreading atmosphere is chilling and lonely.
Hazy streetlights exude no warmth, no welcoming beam.
Muffled footsteps of other lost souls wander to and fro,
They disappear into the void, each in turn seeking some light.
I feel lost in the murky maze of unfamiliar streets,
There are no subtle clues as to where I might be standing.
So I close my eyes, walking slowly one step at a time
My self-imposed blindness befriending me
Moving forward, gaining confidence, regaining self-control.
The air I breathe now feels lighter, drier, warmer.
Slowly the sun breaks through bringing relief from suffocation,
There is a light breeze on my face, rays from the sun on my cheek.
Blindness erased by imagination!

Alzheimer's

One day you just up and left me, I don't know where you are
I thought I saw you yesterday watching from afar
We were so close, inseparable, in unison, as one
But since you've abandoned me, my world has become undone
I gaze steadily at a picture and see a familiar face
Your name now escapes me, my minds a dark and empty space.
I know my husband visited, I'm sure it was yesterday,
But everyone is telling me, it's years since he passed away.
Family told me this would happen as the years went on
My brain's committed adultery, and everything has gone.
I'll sit in this strange place; that they tell me now's my home
Surrounded by so many others yet feeling utterly alone.

The Book

The last time that I saw you, with a smile etched on your face
You laughed mockingly at me, how you needed your own space
Beginning a new chapter, leaving this life behind
Your selfishness took over; you were cruel and so unkind!
To see you now dejected, as your storyline has turned bad
Depleted of all your hopes, so miserable and sad
How did this happen? Where did the plot go wrong?
Now too late you've discovered it's with me that you belong
Your mistake, was the first step, you took away from me
For problems that needed solving, it was I who held the key,
Every choice you believed was yours, was made with my advice,
For each step you took forward, it was me who paid the price.
You struggle now pitifully, wanting to come back
Hoping that I'll revive you with all that you now lack
But I too turned a page and my book is being penned
My Forward is being written for you it is The End!

Moonbeams

You gave me moonbeams in a jar to lovingly light my way
Their opalescence softening, the corners of my day.
Carrying it close to my heart, collecting lovers souvenirs
Constantly moving forward we journeyed through the years
But then one day faltering, I dropped my precious jar
The cut glass wounded me deeply and now I wear a scar.
The floating wisps of the beams spiralled their way back home
I was now left in darkness, feeling abandoned and alone.
Stumbling along on life's dull road not sure how to carry on
Regretting the loss of what I'd been given now that it was gone.
But sometimes I come across those who share their light with me
They make my life brighter because their radiance is free.

The Means to an End

Weary and tired, weathered and worn
Rested the old man haggard, forlorn.
Life had been good to him until late
The roll of the dice had cast his fate
To live without her was too much to bear
Although loving his family, he now didn't care
The only place that he felt less in the dark
Was her favourite bench there in the park.
It was here that they courted in their youth
They pledged their love with a passionate truth,
Here they swore that no matter what
This wooden park bench would be "their spot".
When the days had been hard and the money tight
They would come to sit and plan through the night.
When the children were young they would run and play
And around that same spot their grandchildren stay.
The following day he shuffled back again
With tablets and water to banish the pain
He swallowed with calmness the means to his end
And slowly slipped off to join his best friend.
The park keeper found him, with a smile set in place,
Clutching a picture of his wife's sunny face.
He knew how important memories could be
And knew this old man had now been set free.
He was buried beside her and no tear was shed
For in living they knew he was already dead.

Palette

A true flight of fancy leaving reality behind.
Bursting through thick clouds of cluttered confusion.
I soar to new heights with hope and exhilaration of a fresh start.
Troubles of the past that weighed me down now slip their chains,
I watch them crash into the abyss below.
A fresh palette beckons a master stroke on pure canvas
Passionate blood reds, bursting with energy,
Fresh greens granting me the natural pleasures of life,
Cool blues calmly whisper to me, freedom at last!
I will reinvent my life, redecorate my existence…
Banished are the infuriating dull greys that have been my prison.

Peace

Warming sunlight settled gently, chasing the night away
Painting brightness on my world, in a calm and peaceful way.
Prompted by a delicate breeze, the promise of a hopeful start
I made my way down the stairs with a contented happy heart.
The heavy aroma of coffee and the bite of buttered toast
The simplicity of quiet times is one I value most.
Gazing through the window, observing silent passers by
Everything was in its place, I expelled a contented sigh.

Then hurtled from my dream, a pained siren began to wail
People ran for cover, the sun instantly turned pale.
No movement or sound for a moment, then suddenly a boom,
I viewed the devastation of what was once my room.
Making my way through the concrete, staggering through the mess
The promise of a peaceful day somersaulted into distress.
Empty dust laden streets now held a deathly hush,
Perhaps I shouldn't be deceived by the quiet times so much.

Nothing Left

I'm on the highway to hell; can't you sense it in the air?
Blindly crashing through my life, perilously, without care
Maybe it's the drugs I use, or the reckless speed I drive
Hanging on by a thread, my senses raw, I feel alive.

I'm on the highway to hell; an irreversible dangerous course
Partying hard, hurting others, showing no remorse
How long can I last at this torrid burning pace?
Soon to drown in exhaustion, disappearing without trace.

I'm on the highway to hell; there's no stopping me now
Too late, wanting to turn back, but afraid I don't know how.
And when I have gone I wonder, what trail I'll have left behind.
A tortured voice screams in my mind, "There'll be nothing left to find!"

Shared Senses

Taste the spices giving flavour to your life
Shower others with them as they pass
That they may inhale pungent aromatic warmth
Let them taste what they are missing.

Dress in vibrant silks that give colour to your life
You will shimmer and shine amongst the drab
Cover them with colour to arouse their senses
Let them follow your illuminated path.

Play the music that orchestrates your life
Penetrate their mundane hum, let them hear!
Your music will change their dragging pace
Let them feel the rhythm of a happier existence.

Touch the objects that give feeling to your life
Hold the hardest of stone in the softness of your hands
Show them the gift of strength through sensitivity
Let them touch and be touched.

Taste the fruits of the earth that sustain your life
Be nourished from the seeds you have sown
Move them away from the barren ground
Let them enjoy the bountiful fruits of companionship.

The Four Winds

The four winds now blow in one direction
Hemispheres merge, the poles latch arms
I wait for the earth to stop, to grind to a halt.
Silence.
My world dissolves into nothingness.
I have been here before and know my fate
I'll languish on the bed with my emotions at war
Pain in one corner, frustration in the other,
Refereeing the fight anguish will crown emptiness the victor.
It will rise in all its glory and survey the desolation
Watching as my bleeding heart is hurled
Downwards into the pit of loneliness
There to join others tossed aside before me.

The reality is startling; it's a glorious summer's day
On the window ledge a sparrow hops back and forth,
Whistling a shrill tune at life's abounding glory.
Below, leaves on the yellow rose bush flutter in the breeze
Proud velvet petals release a soft scent into the air.
A single white cloud rests in the blue sky,
I listen to the chatter of children, splashing in the river below.
Warmth from this idyllic scene begins to radiate through my fog
Motionless, I absorb the atmosphere, allowing myself to be soothed.
I'll tend my wounds, dress, and sit on that sunny high ledge
There lean out stretching way beyond my reach,
A futile attempt to pluck the yellow bloom below!

Desertion

The tormenting wind gate-crashes in.
Damp sand sinks below your foot fall
Winter has come and the beach is finally deserted.
Nature runs wild over its empty playground
The dormant grey slate cliffs lay as dragons in wait
Evil lurking below their rough wet surfaces,
They wait to be awakened with the returning tide.
Taste the salt in the air, walk on, the tide is out.
No impediment in your path, no reason to falter
Feel the freedom of emptiness that desertion brings.

Ride of My Life

Waiting for the ride to start, ticket tightly held in my hand
Not sure of my destination, I'm a traveller with no plan
There were only two more adventurers, sometimes glancing my way
They seemed a bit familiar, had I met them before today?
As we journeyed quickly on, I soon became aware
Others now had joined us, a few began to stare.
The ride had picked up greater speed, rocking to and fro
I tried to find a better seat, but there was nowhere for me to go.
The vehicle was now so crowded, I couldn't enjoy the ride
Jostled, pushed and trodden on as I was hurtled from side to side
My parents (the adventurers) left; I had to manage all alone…
The ride's a reflection of my life, a wild ride far from home.

You're My Bookend Lover

I watch you watching me from afar
Parted by a world of drama and comedy
Philosophy and religion
Between us the distance forever changing
Well suited apart, yet needing each other to feel complete
Your strength my weakness, your weakness my strength
As the years pass the gap widens,
But we hold each other in our sights
Destined to lean on each other
Limited editions with our own shelf lives.

SOS

The train's left the station and there's no way to get home
Your cell phone's lost; you're feeling scared, frightened and alone
Cut off from all familiar things, everything feels weird
You'd better sit on the bench until your head has cleared.
The party went on far too long and you lost the track of time
Too much food, too many drugs and way too much cheap wine
Aware of a stranger at your side you jump up with a start
You can hear heavy breathing and the pumping of your heart
No matter how fast you run they seem to match your pace
You need to increase your step if you want to leave this place
Tripping up as you run, crashing to the ground
Caught among the bushes; knowing for sure you will be found
Everything's now gone black; your body's wracked with pain
Deafening screams convince you that you've finally gone insane.
No missed train, no party, just drugs and cheap red wine
Again you've collapsed helplessly, for the umpteenth time.
Your conscience was the stranger who clawing at your mind
Tried to save you, from yourself, for this, the very last time.

To and Fro

Standing behind the picket fence I surveyed my future,
Should I step out and embrace a new beginning?
Leave behind the comfortable confines of security?
The gate reluctantly swung open, so I passed through.
Glancing back one last time I saw it had not completely shut
It beckoned me back to safety, creaking gently to and fro.
The die had been cast and I moved forward to meet my destiny
Tempted into the orchard of life I ate the fruit of independence.
Blinded by the unspoken promise of success, gathering momentum,
Forging forward, greater strides, curious to meet the unknown.
Too much too soon, I had taken one step too far
Sinking into the quicksand of greed and selfishness.
As the darkness drew me in with its suffocating grip
The only sound, a distant crash of a slamming gate!

Brimming

So, you say my "cup runneth over"
But with what has it been filled?
A draft quenching my thirst for excitement?
Or a heavy potion, that leaves a cloying after taste?
Those around me say I have it all.
By whose measure is that?
But I will drink with gusto,
Lap up each drop of life,
Tasting bitterness and sweetness with each mouthful,
Leaving my head in a constant daze
However filled, when drained I will be left empty.

Fountain

Bathing in the fountain of my youth,
I'm refreshed by a deluge of memories
The clear waters of nostalgia gleam,
Reflecting upon my once smooth skin.
Bursting spray flashes around me,
Illuminating visions from the past.
Now with the closing of the years,
The fountain's image has transformed,
An abandoned deep well sits in its place,
Filled with misspent years,
The water darker, still reflective,
But the energy depleted and still.

Super Dad

At 5; my Dad's a super hero I know this to be true
Whenever I have a problem he'll know just what to do
He may not have super powers, or disappear in a wink
But I know his abilities are mighty when he's had a drink.

At 16; my Dad he's a tower of strength; he knows just how to fight
If I disturb him during the football, he'll hit me with such might
He doesn't mean to hurt me; it's just his drunken way
Better he goes out at night and sleep straight through the day.

At 40; my Dad doesn't seem to remember, why I never call
I think he suffered brain damage from a drunken fall
Maybe if I smile at him his memory will return
Of how I idolized him and for his attention yearn.

At 60; now that he has passed away it really makes me sad
The super hero had his faults, but still he was my Dad
Life had not been easy, he did what he thought was best
His cape had torn, his mask had slipped, but at last he now can rest.

Freedom

What freedom! What a carefree life!
Whilst others suffocate with responsibilities
The weight of a vexatious life bearing down on them
He has no worries and no peer pressure.
He can breathe in the dawn's new air
Watching with curious interest.
Commuters spill into a hole in the ground
Like water flowing helplessly into a drain
As others are spewed out already tired and weary
Yet their day has barely begun!
He is not bound by time, money or motion
Contented, he slips back into his cardboard box by the pier
Homeless but happy, he is master of his day.

Hollywood Heroes Die

Riding the fast track to heaven, hurtling at great speed
Blinkered from my surroundings, a yearning to be freed
Volleying blindly forward, fleeing the human race
My self-destruction a la carte, at a lightening pace.

Finally I've made it through, achieved my ultimate goal
Guillotined from my life, at one now with my soul
No pressures, no pain, or sorrow, just a simple peace
A happy numbness and lightness, a merciful release.

Watching them put me in the ground, on a sunny day
Some of them astounded that I took my life this way.
Unaware my existence was just a theatrical sham
Suffering from depression, never free to be who I am.

But those who truly loved me, will understand my choice
A life of constant pained screaming, with a silent voice
Maybe they'll be happy one day, when they think of me,
And my journey to a place where I was truly meant to be.

The Comforter

I never believed that you'd return, and come to sit with me,
Having parted years ago, not knowing what would be
Coming downstairs to find you, waiting at my door
Shocked, but filled with pleasure as you walked across the floor.
Sitting by the fire side, we hugged in the warming glow
I caught my breath and eventually whispered a "hello"
You smiled at me knowingly, no need to say a word
Understanding just how much, my feelings had been stirred.
When I awoke the fire had died, you'd abandoned me again
It was just your ghost who'd visited, comforting me in my pain
I'll start the day alone again, wishing the day away
So I can meet you in the night for your transitory stay.

Wise Words

"Better to have loved and lost than never to have loved at all"
What heartless wit? What foolish mind? Whoever had the gall?
With such a cruel and naïve thought, my life fashioned to that creed
I have to tend my broken heart and root out that worthless seed.

Abandoned by my lover, I'm left trembling in his wake
The total loss, the emptiness, it was all one big mistake
Now I've learned it's not the truth and to my greatest cost
Whoever wrote those fatal words has never loved or lost!

Chocolate Box

Walking in your footsteps I stumbled.
Lying on the ground I'm looking up at the sky
A picture perfect chocolate box
Marshmallow clouds, a yellow jelly sun.
I sense you've carried on without me.
Alone on the path I am motionless
I close my eyes and hear a rumble
Something ominous is on the path
The brown earth around me vibrates
Specks of chocolate jump up in a dance
The earth is drumming its tune
I hear muffled voices in the distance
Others must be approaching
Most will not see me on the ground
Those that do, just step over me
There is no helping hand to guide me on
Walking in your footsteps I now understand
The ground is awaiting my footfall
I'll tread my own sweet path.

Re-Gifting

The greatest gift you gave me,
I now give back to you
Having recklessly wasted it,
I've re-packaged it anew
It may look very familiar,
An echo from the past
Now I'm returning it to you,
So it may be used properly at last!
You bestowed upon me freedom,
A beautiful and rare thing
But I abused it very badly and
Was wounded by life's sting
It came with no instructions,
No warning for me to heed
So I just used it carelessly,
In mind, in thought, and deed
One's not supposed to re-gift,
But now I understand
The meaning of what you gave
So freely with your hand
It would make me happy
If I could give it back to you
You'll cherish its value deeply,
And know with it what to do.
You may decide to pass it on
To a more deserving friend
But I beg you this time guide them,
So they'll have a happier end.

Stand Up and be Counted

Turn away from the homeless man
Just walk the other way
Forget about his dreadful looks
His teeth rotting with decay.
No need to watch him beg for food
Why feel sorry for his plight
If he stopped drinking alcohol
His life could be alright.
Walk away and block out the thought
Of how some people live
He'd only squander the copper coins
If you decided you should give.
But don't assume it's his entire fault
That his life is just a waste
You don't know how he got here
Or what choices that he'd faced.
Be brave and turn to face him
Maybe there's something you could do
Be more generous with your time
One day this could be you!

Gravestone

Looking at the headstone I couldn't understand
How a piece of chiselled stone could do justice to a man
When a child he had to bear his poverty with pain
Then as a man burdened, embarrassed by the shame.
He and his soul mate had managed to make ends meet
Despite the poor job offers he would not succumb to defeat
He worked until exhausted yet still trying to do more
Providing for his family, keeping hunger from their door.
His life was hard; his children grew and had children of their own
And now all that is left of him is this grey and dismal stone
Looking at the grave again I couldn't understand
How a piece of chiselled stone could do justice to a man.

Muddy Waters

Stare deep into the cloudy pool beyond your reflection
Can you see through to the clear waters of happiness?
Cleanse the heartache from your weary body
Ignore the stranger's pebble cast from behind
It will confuse the still waters mudding them for a while,
Wait patiently for the ripples to slowly subside
Watch the tormentor drown and tranquillity will return.

On Weakness

Close your eyes and imagine a different kind of life
One of peace and happiness, no worries and no strife
Close your eyes and imagine this calm and quiet place
One of sweet dreams, and loving, the smile of a friendly face.
Lay there, imagine its tranquillity, let your body float away
A warm sublime happiness that could now make up your day
This place is much nearer, so much closer than you think
It only takes another drag, another stiff long drink.

Grind

Morning comes again; another work day unfolds into another.
Warm coffee sweetened to relieve the bland taste of routine
Rush hour companions absorbed in their own deep confusion.
Different newspapers, the same pictures the same stories!
Somebody coughs nudging you back into reality.
You dive again into the sea of words reporting another disaster
Carried forward, swept towards the glass prison of your existence.
Papers to process, contracts to read, endless reports to complete
Each file replaced by another intruder until the day ends.
Not a moment too soon into the depths of the metro you plunge again
Emerging at your door, worn, tired and numb...
There the morning's empty coffee cup sits accusingly
A familiar reminder of tomorrow's yesterday.

The Tramp

As the street light on the corner casts its hazy shadow,
A lonesome figure falters beneath the diluted glow
From where will he draw the strength to stay outside?
He is alone standing under a menacing shroud of winter.
Beckoning firelight seeps through drawn curtains
A flickering image of the past settles in his mind
He is a changed man...
Life's battles have chiselled down his existence
Yearning for some shelter, a need to feel human again.
Trudging onwards warming himself with memories,
The ghosts of his children dance ahead smiling back at him
Their echoing laughter fading as they leave him behind
His only companion the bitter wind blowing in another lonely day,
A mere continuance of his solitary sojourn through his life's hell.

Happiness at Home

The traveller sunk to the ground beneath the shady trees
Head hung low, feeling empty, he crumpled on his knees
But he knew he'd have to carry on, despite the heavy pain
He had to reclaim what he'd lost and be with her again.
He'd married young and never knew that love was not her concern
She'd seen how much wealth he had and let their money burn.
The more he made the more she spent, she literally made him pay
Until with his strength depleted, he just had to get away.
The years had left him lonely; they had worn him to the bone
But despite the coldness that she'd shown, with her, he was not alone
Mustering up all his strength he headed towards her door
He'd give her everything of himself until he had no more.

Under Pressure

Slow down a while; you need a break
Empty your mind, your health's at stake
Flirting the boundaries of insanity
Too many pressures that others can't see
They think that you're fine, that your life's a breeze
So they assume, as always, you'll cope with ease
But gnawing away from the inside
The pain's running out of places to hide
Emotionally threadbare, dissolving away
A machine of a human stuck on replay.

CHAPTER TWO

LIGHT

The Boss

The family gathered together, eager for the will to be read
Inheritance the only concern running through each head
Congregated silently to mourn, their sudden, sad loss
Illness having taken Papa, their powerful Mafia Boss.

Sophia his wife sobbed, a tear rolled down from one eye
Whilst Ricardo the frustrated son, expelled a dramatic sigh
Uncles and Aunts hopeful, and the greedy cousins curious too
Waiting to hear if they'd get, what they felt they rightfully were due.

The lawyer fidgeted uncomfortably, and slowly began to read
The atmosphere was heavy, filled with tension and greed
They all listened intently, until he read to the end of the will
It then began to dawn on them, they would all be getting nil!

The Boss at the time of writing, being of sound body and mind
Had decided that now was the time, to pay them back in kind
He had always taken care of them, throughout his long life
Giving only the best to his poor long suffering wife

His son despite being troublesome, was always looked after well
The recklessness, booze and drugs, as well as the gambling hell
All trying to take advantage, throughout most of his life
The lying and the cheating, he'd known had always been rife.

Where was the fortune he'd amassed? Nobody had any clue
They looked helplessly at each other, not knowing what to do.
As the preacher ended the service they got up and started to leave
The anger of inheriting no money was making it hard to breathe.

The coffin soon to be cremated, was simple and made of pine
The handles were rough hemp or some inferior kind of twine.
The Boss, who was not stupid, and knew he was going to hell
Gave instructions to fill the coffin, with him and his money as well!

My Ex

You're like an ill-fitting coat giving bad cover
Measuring up short, as an ideal lover.
Draped on my shoulders, a long baggy fit
Just like you it will never commit
Pathetic long sleeves flapping around
With Neanderthal knuckles that scrape the ground.
Keeping me dangling as a button hanging loose
A belt with no loops you're of such little use!
So the time has come to give you away
Let some other idiot hang you out on display.

Sun Down / Sun Up

As the tide rolls in and the sand disappears
Your mind struggles wildly to recapture lost years
Thoughts silently submerged in the current below
No longer in sight, erased by the flow
Cast your eyes upwards to the warm setting sun
Igniting the memories to where your thoughts run
Next morning will stretch out its beckoning hand
Calling you back for a stroll on fresh sand.

A Tired Man's Woes

I was just so very tired; I couldn't get up today
Despite a loud alarm clock, that helps me start my day
I ate my breakfast bleary eyed, dozed off over my toast
Stumbled my way to the door, tripped over all the post
At the bus stop I fell asleep and missed the bus at eight
It was only waking later, I realized I was late
Vaguely hearing some chatting of a person next to me
He was banging on about something…whatever could it be?
At my desk I snored again, disturbed by the all the chatter
These people they just bothered me with their constant natter!
Maybe they were trying to tell me, something I should know
But my attention span was limited, my brain was reacting slow
When I shuffled round the office, they all began to snicker
Was it because I couldn't manage, to walk around any quicker?
The day had passed hearing mumbles of the odd passers-by,
I just couldn't seem to wake up, not even open one eye
So many people bothering me with such inaudible stuff
By the time it got to 4 o' clock I knew I'd had enough
Somehow I managed to get home, making it through the door
A snack was all I could swallow; I had no strength for more
Whatever they were trying to tell me, was in my head a jumbled mess
Then looking in the mirror saw, I was wearing my wife's dress!

Order

The Judge began scowling and made a tutting sound
The accused started whistling, tapping his foot on the ground
His lordship demanded silence, the convict was creating hell
Or in contempt of court, he'd be sent back to his cell
The angry Judge began to glare but it didn't change a thing
The damn defiant criminal had now begun to sing
His councillor told his client this would put him in a plight
If he carried on like this it would obviously take all night
Not put off by the Judge he continued his annoying song
When would this be over it was dragging on too long!
The time had come to put a stop, to the criminal's show
His Lordship banged his gavel and sent him back below
The happy criminal left (having pushed the Judge to his limit,
His Lordship unaware in the cell, was the con's conjugal visit).

Someone Out There

There must be someone out there; we can't be the only ones
Living here on this little globe under a burning sun
We must go and investigate and find some other life
Maybe their world is peaceful, free of wars and strife
I know it sounds a bit far-fetched, but think on it for a minute
If we exist in the universe, why can't there be others in it?
We've sent out signals with a hope that some aliens will hear
It would be so exciting if they would enter our atmosphere,
We'd exchange ideas and hopes, learn new things as well
How we each live our lives, there'd be an awful lot to tell.
Maybe though, they might be scared, to venture out and be seen
They may not like our skin colour, we call it Martian green.

Who is She?

Standing at the bus stop I thought that I could see
Another woman with him, whoever could it be?
I know his wife is away, but that is no excuse
I'll have to go and confront him, what story will be his ruse?
Should I call and tell her, that he is a cheating rat?
She could threaten to divorce him. It'll put an end to that!
Perhaps it's not my business; they don't seem to want to hide
Maybe ignorance really is bliss, (so's a little on the side)
It's no good I can't ignore it; I'll have to seek her out
Tell her he's with a floozy, who's putting it about!
She must be back from her trip in a day or two
That will give me time, to think what I should do
I called to check she was in; she was keen for me to come
I'm sure that she'll be less keen; when she finds out he is a bum
As she opened up the door, you could have bowled me over
That hussy was my good friend; she'd had a head to toe makeover!

Truth

I tripped over Truth, sitting in the middle of my path
It sat there smirking at me, and gave a knowing laugh
"How could you not see me, an obstacle in your way?
I'm loud and I should be, clear as the light of day!

Traveling along in your thick fog, oblivious of me
Selfishness having blinded you, so me you didn't see!
Now that we have finally met, please look at me again
At all the problems that arise, there's nothing left to gain.

You must retreat and start afresh, this time tell the truth
Look back hard and try to correct the errors of your youth
It won't be easy to admit the lies; it's hard to say *"I'm sorry"*
But now it's time to apologize and not the time to worry.

There may be those who won't forgive, others not forget
For every little lie you told you owe them now a debt
It's your last chance to heed my words before it's all too late!
Take on responsibility; relieve your conscience of the weight"

I looked down hard at the ground, Truth had spoken long
It was time to consider, where I had gone wrong?
The only thing left for me to do was kick it in the head
No one need know the truth as Truth was knocked down dead!

The Hunter

Searching for a strategic spot the hunter hid away
Determined to bag a tasty catch, by the end of day
Waiting very quietly, hungry to "have a go"
Blending in to fool his prey so they would never know
After giving a quick glance, a creature ventured near
Taking a drink to quench her thirst stifling her fear
When quite sated looking up she then became aware
His hungry eyes locked on hers, they both began to stare
She turned her back panicking and quickly ran away
Leaving him hanging back to find some other prey
Blending back into the background, he again began to spy
There is nothing worse for a girl, than a lecherous barfly.

Sweet Old Lady

A broken window hung in its frame,
The paint chipped off the door,
The abandoned house in our street
No longer a home any more.
There was an old woman, who lived there,
She just disappeared one day!
Nobody knew what happened,
And why she left that way.
She always seemed so cheery,
Had a warm and welcoming smile
One couldn't pass her in the street
Without stopping, to chat for a while.
Such a great house full of intrigue!
Like an old curiosity shop
A wonderfully old fashioned kitchen,
With an authentic butchers block
Rows of bottles on the shelves,
Filled with wondrous things,
Tiers of neatly jarred goodies
All packed with flavourings.
The garden, now overgrown,
With all the weeds running wild
A quaint shed in the corner,
Stacked with gardening tools inside.
But there are things we didn't know
Some events are best left untold,
Horrific deeds and nightmarish things
That would make your blood run cold
This little woman with that smile,
With that glint in her eye
Was not as pleasant as she seemed,
And here's the reason why
She was a big meat eater,
Relishing it fresh and raw
Tempting dogs and stray cats in,
She enjoyed a juicy paw
The tools in the gardening shed,
Did more than prune the odd rose

It turns out the jars in the kitchen,
Contained left over animal toes!
The last time that we saw her was
With a Rottweiler on a lead
He was pulling her into the house,
At a salivating speed
Did she try and chop him up,
And eat him for her dinner?
Or did he get his revenge,
And devour that despicable sinner?

Spot

I had a nasty spot, big and red and horrid
Of all the places to break out! In the middle of my forehead!
As if this wasn't enough, people's eyes just tended to linger
Telling me I had a spot and pointing with their finger
It made me so embarrassed I lowered my head a bit
Did they think I was unaware and have to point at it?
I had a eureka moment, "I'll cover it with a plaster"
That just made it more obvious, what a big disaster!
My Mother said *"don't touch it you'll end up making it worse
Instead of getting better the result will be the reverse"*
Despite the good advice she gave I thought I'd have a dig
My goodness…it's now a crater; how did it get that big?

Liar!

I dug myself into a hole of pathetic deep deceit
The overt lie like mud clung around my feet
Dragging me down deeper still, each word became a curse
I tried to extricate myself, but it made the whole thing worse
You start out with a little lie then soon begin to sink
At first the rush is thrilling, until you hit the brink!
So next time that you're quizzed, "have you forgotten my name"?
It is best to say yes and be honest; it will save the ensuing shame.

On Tears

I cried so hard in such pain
Tears streamed down like heavy rain
My body sore, I hurt and ached
The torture clear, make no mistake
I sunk to the ground and felt so weak,
Shaking and trembling, couldn't speak
It was the funniest joke I ever heard
To laugh so much was not absurd.

Wishing Well

I flipped a coin over my head into the wishing well
Desperately wishing for many things, hoping to ignite a spell
Naturally wishing for myself, years of continued good health
And I suppose I should admit it, an increase in my wealth
I wished for love, and happiness, some peace, an elusive word!
That coin's got its work cut out if my wishes are to be heard
As I sat there wishing, you may have heard an echoed cry
My last coin had been wasted as the well was completely dry!

The Fortune Teller

The mystical sign on her tent tempted me to find out more
In the swirling magical mist what was it that she saw?
As the fortune teller gazed into her cloudy crystal ball
I didn't like her expression a bit, no no not at all

Should I interrupt her pained and contorted face?
Or just get up and leave this strange and creepy place?
Was it such a good idea to find out what's in store?
Maybe there are evil things lurking at my door…

I'd crossed her palm with silver and waited for her read
But with her anguished twisted face I wanted to recede
Despite that I waited patiently for her to use her mystic art
Only to discover her pain was wind, as she let out a mighty fart!

Professionalism

The undertaker had had enough of being with the dead
And tried to think of a profession, that he might prefer instead

How about a pilot? Jetting people through the sky?
But then thought… not a good idea, if we crash they all would die!

Maybe a master baker? Baking delicious pies
But food poisoning is a danger; I'd be the cause of their demise

Perhaps then a ship's captain? What could go wrong with this?
But what about the icebergs? They could die in the abyss

Hey! How about a doctor? Treating sick patients all day
But he then rejected that idea, as they'd eventually pass away

Maybe I'll stick with what I do; it may not be much fun
But that way I won't have to worry, I won't be killing anyone!

1960s

Where is the old washing line, strung from post to tree?
The wooden prop the wooden pegs, the way things used to be
Red melamine cups in the kitchen, squares of linoleum on the floor
That familiar smell of cooking when we walked in through the door
The airing cupboard with wooden shelves piled with sheets of cotton
Soft and scented bath towels are something I've not forgotten
A pantry stacked high with food, the scullery with its big old sink
The cellar filled with many things but mainly Grandpa's drink
I don't think it really matters how much time will pass
There's a comfort in recalling the happy days of our past.

The Psychiatrist's Misery

It's just been one of those days! I should have stayed in bed!
The patients coming for sessions seem to get inside *my* head
I really should have not left home, just stayed well away
How glorious to disappear, just for one short day…
They *really* are so boring and I'm *really* not in the mood
Continually pushing me to the brink so I end up being rude!
Isn't it enough I've acquiesced, to say a brief "*hello*"?
Who has the patience for them, and their boring, relentless, flow?
I'm not interested in their troubles, or their worries, come to that
They just plonk themselves on my couch and want a little chat!
I too have lots of problems! I honestly don't need theirs
So what if their husbands have run off… seriously? … Who cares?
They share with me such rubbish about their petty little lives
If they've come to me for sympathy they'll be in for a nasty surprise
Their inner feelings they reveal are such a monumental bore
Then they'll come back the following week and pour out even more!
I think I'll change to taxidermy, goodness how I'd feel chuffed
As when they knocked on my door I could tell them to get stuffed

Constructive Criticism

You say its constructive criticism. I just think you're rude!
Posturing with false concern doesn't prove you're shrewd
Radiating a spreading smile, airing your complaint
Looking concerned and interested, invoking no constraint
"I only want to help you", a shallow thing to say
After pulling me apart in a damning critical way
Suggesting how you think, I should then proceed instead,
Using barbed words of criticism that penetrate my head
Please don't think I'm sensitive or easily take offense
It's just "constructive criticism" as a tool, is a rude pretence!

Boredom

The teacher woke me from my sleep how dare she interrupt!
Her droning was so tedious my eyes just seemed to shut
It wasn't that she saw me, but because she was such a bore,
She must have caught on to me as I erupted with a snore.

Sitting up as though I knew, exactly what chapter we'd reached
I pretended to be attentive in the lesson as she preached
When again she turned away I drifted back into my dream
Then woke to find the bell had rung, there was no one to be seen.

I had to write lines on the board "*I must not snore in class*"
She didn't seem to care it was another boring task!
The teacher gave me a letter, so my parents would know the score
But as they reached the second line they too began to snore!

Burn Baby Burn

There is something in the air I wonder where it's from?
A sort of burning, rubber smell, the kind that lingers on
Maybe it's from my flat mate's room, although I am not sure
I'd better go upstairs to check and knock hard on his door
I banged quite loud and yelled to him but he did not reply
He must be in real trouble! Surely that's the reason why.
I opened the door, looked around, there was nothing there to see
What the hell was going on and where the hell was he?
Then suddenly I sniffed the whiff from the bathroom door
What on earth was he doing? There was water on the floor!
I dashed straight in and to my surprise he was crying in the bath
It took all the strength I had not to burst out with a laugh
This grown up man was whimpering sadly like a boy
Because the radiator had melted his rubber ducky toy!

The Secret's Out!

How did they know where we were and what I had to eat?
Where we sat to have a chat and who else I was to meet?
I don't understand how they knew it really makes me mad
I hadn't told a soul, and I didn't think you had!
The secret's out it can't be denied our photo's on display
You can see us plainly laughing, clear in the light of day
Why were we of such interest? So many people can now look
I'm shared, liked and commented about on a page of damn Facebook!

Health Food?

Maybe my glass is half full; it's hard from here to tell
I'm on the floor drunk again, I truly feel unwell
I remember going out last night and having just one or two
But now my head is spinning and my head's stuck down the loo
Maybe they spiked my vodka with drugs or a few small pills
Why else would I feel so bad and green around the gills?
Wait!
Maybe it was my supper; I tried a new diet health drink
Maybe all that healthy stuff isn't as healthy as you think
To hell with all the dieting and the pressure to be thin
That box of healthy nutritious drinks is now going in the bin!

Future

Looking down into the cup, observing I could see
Coffee grounds predicting, exactly what was to be.
The future was dark and messy; that I could read for sure
So ordered another cup as I needed to see some more
Maybe this time there'd be a change and things will look just great
A more positive outcome would be a preferred kind of fate.
I took a slurp, jumping up, as harsh expletives sprung
The drink I gulped was way too hot, and it had burnt my tongue
Now in pain, I really don't care *exactly* what will be
I'll be contented with my lot and in future drink iced tea!

The King's Game

The King was sitting on his throne thinking *"life is such a bore!*
There's more to life than riches, there's something I want more"!
He perversely divided his wealth between his wife and son
But as he divvied up the cash was when trouble had begun
The Queen received all the jewels and most of the cash too
The Prince was given a pittance. What's a boy to do?
He pleaded with his father that this *"wasn't very fair"*
As when the king popped his clogs he'd be the only heir
The Queen wasn't bothered saying *"every man for himself*
And speaking as a Mother, my concerns only for your health".
That made the Prince angry, he felt he deserved much more,
He scratched his head and thought, how to settle the score?
Suddenly it hit him, and he devised a sneaky plan
It would render her quite helpless and make him a richer man.
He told the King that his mother had always been untrue
"In fact she's down right scandalous, a cunning little shrew"
The King flew into a frenzied fit he gobbled up the lie
"How could you have been unfaithful? ...Never mind the why "!
Furious at the Queen, he then reclaimed all his money
The Prince in the corner thought *"now this is what I call funny"*
Then the Queen was banished, sent away in only what she wore,
"It's all untrue" she screeched until she was heard no more
The Prince still in the corner feeling somewhat bad
Had it been a wise thing to make his father mad?
Still, there was the inheritance; he was now bound to get for sure
He went to the King's bed chamber and knocked upon the door
"Father I'm sorry to upset you so, but now you surely see
Your money would be well invested, if you gave it now to me"
The King turned round and winked with a twinkle in his eye
"Don't you think that I knew the whole thing was a lie?
For years I've wanted rid of her and you gave me an excuse
You've been a great service to me, but now you're of no use
You can now go and join her in some kingdom far away
The money I will keep for now and the jewels with me can stay
My lover can now move in with me, to her I've pledged my heart
We can live happily in this castle and have a brand new start"

Doctor's Advice

The doctor took another look, he couldn't believe his eyes
In all his years doctoring this was his first one of such a size
"How do you manage to conduct your life"? He asked with dismay
"Don't you find it bothersome, it must get in the way"!
The patient turned bright red, embarrassed at his plight
It's true the thing was quite large and bothered him at night
"The only thing you can do, if you want to improve your life
Is to go and see your lawyer and divorce your big fat wife"!

Gossip

I overheard them talking, they seemed to be discussing me
That my behaviour didn't suit them, and what a pest I could be.
I moved a little closer so as not to miss a word,
But they moved to another corner and so could not to be heard!
Continuing their whispering I decided to again move near
Wanting to gain some ground, so that I could hear.
I didn't see it coming they had been oh so very sly
Beware the swat of a newspaper when you are a fly

Lovers' Games

Don't try and play that game with me, don't try and catch me out!
Be my ladder not my snake; don't cause me to give doubt
Deal the cards out evenly for a chance of a winning hand,
Keep the Jokers for yourself; don't trump me as you planned!
I used to play solitaire, fill in crosswords on my own
And thought having a playmate, would make a happier home
But I've found that when you play, on me you always cheat
Casting the dice with a poker face, smug with your deceit
So back I go to solitaire, no playmates anymore
Being in control of the game; I'll win now that's for sure!

Left or Right

I'm standing at a the junction of a long and weary trail
Having used all my strength to get here; I'm determined not to fail
If I go to my left I see a bumpy, dangerous street
To the right it's narrow with the signposts of defeat
I know I have to decide which is my best track
I've pondered hard, given thought; I think that I'll go back

It's Hell in Heaven

I'm stuck up here in heaven
I suppose it's my own fault
I should have been much naughtier
And maybe gotten caught
So what of fire and brimstone
And the lashing of the flames
I'd rather be down there with friends
Having fun and games.

The Debutante Dress

I spent a fortune on my dress it glittered and it shone,
Amazing! So glamorous! I couldn't wait to put it on.
I'm sure it's worth the huge amount that I had to pay,
To be "the belle of the ball" would really make my day.
I put it on carefully, so as not to damage the dress
Admiring the crystal beads, it will be such a success!
I'd even spent a little more than the original ticketed price,
Buying some extra lace, at the assistant's sound advice.

The stylish skirt swished around, as we circled the ballroom floor,
They all turned green with envy, as each in turn dropped a jaw
Being so hot on the dance floor we stepped outside for a chat,
The evening breeze was cooling; we talked of this and that
Returning to the ballroom, they all turned and grinned at us
Such a gorgeous dress! Who wouldn't make a fuss?
The reason why they were grinning so, wasn't clear to me as yet
Until I looked behind to see the bench paint had been wet!

Do as You're Told

Should I follow parental advice?
Keep away from things of vice
The day will turn into a total bore
But keep me well within the law
I'll be so good and sweet and kind
It'll drive me totally out of my mind
No sex, no drugs and no strong drink
How can any human think?
There must be a kind of midway path
That will make me happy, make me laugh
A small dose of it all must be the stuff
And hope I know when I've had enough!

Heavenly

Waiting on the bench patiently, outside the Pearly Gates
There I spotted two rows down one of my old school mates
I say "mates", but that's not true, I just needed a word to rhyme
He was in fact a lout, who bullied me all the time!

Obviously there's something wrong, he should have gone below
I was brought up believing, if you're evil, that is where you go!
I'll chat with the Head Angel; he'll reward me with no doubt,
They should know that he's been wicked, no need to drag it out.

I found the one with largest harp and tugged on his large white wing
"Are you aware there's an impostor here; do you know the trouble he'll bring?
I'm sure they're waiting down in Hell; you'd better send him away
There he'll have accomplices they can bully each other all day"

The angel smiled and looked at me; a reward was coming my way
I felt sure there'd be an upgrade, and I'd be treated well during my stay!
To my horror it was me cast out, and after tumbling from the skies
I found myself at the mouth of Hell, upset and with much surprise

Later whilst warming up I heard the angel's far off voice
"You had your chance, but blew it, you left me little choice
He was there to test your goodness, to see how your soul's inclined
You are not worthy enough for Heaven you're vengeful and unkind"

Blind as a Bat

Why do they make print so small?
It doesn't make much sense at all
I have usually found that it means
There is danger hidden behind the scenes
The little extras that they add
Must stop the food from tasting bad
If we read what's hidden deep within
We'd no doubt throw it in the bin
Type on contracts is so much worse
Doctor's letters are just a curse
Why is there so much for them to hide
Aren't they supposed to be on my side?
So it's off to the optician for me
Maybe he can help me to see…
But I was so disappointed to be told
My eyes are bad, I'm getting old
The eye chart was just a terrible blur
I'll be prescribed thick lenses that's for sure!
So now that I can see much better
Decipher and discern every letter
I've concluded its better not to see
How everyone's blatantly conning me.

Silent Movies

The flickering picture on the screen, black and white no sound
Mundane music imitating hooves riding over ground
The wicked robber stops the coach, the music gathers speed
Watching characters gesticulate, as the starlet takes the lead
But when the camera stops rolling, and the props are put away
The actors aren't as great as the characters that they portray.
Their lives are also black and white, rarely tinged with grey
All depending if they work, if there's money to eat that day.
The only one that's in demand, is well prepared, fed and able
No audition, no lines, no make-up, he just waits around in his stable.

Teamwork

"Be a team member; always give of your best
Don't worry there's no effort, put in by the rest"
But on the day of reckoning, awaiting your reward
You'll not get your wings glued on, by the Almighty Lord
He will be disappointed, as from his point of view
You let the other team members walk all over you
The lesson you should learn from this, is join in with the group
And contribute no more, nor less, than your lazy troupe!

Scotch for the Scotsman

A Scotsman and an Englishman sat down to have a drink
The Scotsman ordered water, which made the Englishman think!
Did the whiskey the barman stock really taste so bad?
Or had his friend the Scotsman gone teetotal raving mad?
The Englishman drank the whiskey and lost his attention span
The Scotsman now snickered because all was going to plan
The whiskey was very good so he had another drink
Ordering more, and then another until he couldn't think
With the Englishman now drunk, the Scotsman had his way
He ordered a bottle for himself and made his drunk friend pay!

Who Needs Them?

I've never had that many friends; I find people such a bore
They tend to be so demanding and always wanting more
There were a few that seemed ok, but what a waste of time!
After all my "giving" left, without reason, without rhyme.
So now I always shun people, if they ever come near
(Although outwardly if unavoidable, pretend to love them dear)
There's just one conclusion to this plight and this is what must be
The only close friends I'll now have, are I myself and me!

Beautiful Creature

My Mother says I'm beautiful, but I know it isn't true
Still, she tries to encourage me (that's what mothers do),
Why was I born so ugly, everyone's so unkind!
Mother says *"don't worry, they say that love is blind"*
I've tried to make some improvements to the way I am
Carry myself upright; hold my stomach in when I can.
Maybe my size puts them off; I'll have to lose some weight
Perhaps then I'll be more alluring, and maybe get a date
That didn't really work too well; I'm hungry all the time
What's another little snack? Is eating such a crime?
I'll bandy round the saying *"I'm fat but I am happy"*
Even though deep down inside I just feel sad and crappy!
Maybe it would help, to hide under a stylish wig,
But the mud around my trotters is a give-away I am a pig.

Internet Advice

Feeling under the weather I thought that I would see
If an internet search of symptoms could find a cure for me.
I found an interesting item, the symptoms seemed to fit
But as I read further down it scared me… just a bit.
Apparently my time's limited, I'd better make a will
It seems there's nothing they can do, no medicine or no pill.
So I closed down my computer and crept off in to bed
Visions of my demise now bouncing around my head.
The symptoms disappeared, but the fear won't go away
I read what can happen; things can change within a day!
I'd diagnosed myself, fearing some medical test
Could an internet search, honestly know what's best?
Years later always worried, I've now lost so much time
Let this be a warning, disregard advice online.

Man of my Dreams

Before we married he seemed like a prince
But now I can only look and wince
After we'd wed he began to change
Things started happening that were strange

As for my existence? He's hardly aware
For all he does is just sit and stare
And when he does eventually speak
Lingering in the air hangs an awful reek

His clothes, I recall, were really smart
Such dashing looks stole my heart
I miss those days from long ago
When he was my attractive beau!

Now he won't even wear a shirt
He looks so grimy, covered in dirt
There's a beady look now in his eyes
He seems more interested in the flies!

I'd always felt that he was tall
Now he stoops and looks so small
Gone his pallor of a healthy glow
A greenish complexion's begun to show

Our fairy tale marriage was born in hell
He's lost all interest in me I can tell
Sitting outside on that rotting log
My prince had turned into a frog!

The Fisherman

The fisherman sat at the edge of his boat
He could see the fish admiring his float
Without moving a muscle he sat there still
Hoping for a bite with all his will.

The fish eyed the man from the sea
Horrified to think what his fate might be
How could he still get to eat the bait
Without landing up on the fisherman's plate?

The fish then made a grab at the float
The man dashed forward from the boat
He put his hand forth to grasp his catch
But this silly fisherman had met his match

The electric eel who had agreed to help
Had shocked his hand and made him yelp
He dropped the fish back into the sea
And the fish and the eel had caught their tea.

Pot of Gold

I've reached the rainbows end, yet see no pot of gold
No chest of riches or glittering coins, nothing I can hold!
Maybe the tranquillity here's a better measure of wealth,
The silence and the peace, a pure treasure in itself